PARABLES & FAXES

PARABLES
& FAXES

Gwyneth Lewis

BLOODAXE BOOKS

First published 1995 by
Bloodaxe Books Ltd,
P.O. Box 1SN,
Newcastle upon Tyne NE99 1SN.

Bloodaxe Books Ltd acknowledges
the financial assistance of Northern Arts.

Cover printing by J. Thomson Colour Printers Ltd, Glasgow.

Printed in Great Britain by
Bell & Bain Limited, Glasgow, Scotland.

To L.D.D.,
with love

Acknowledgements

Acknowledgements are due to the editors of the following publications in which some of these poems first appeared: *As Girls Could Boast* (The Oscars Press, 1994), *The Gregory Anthology 1987-1990* (Hutchinson, 1990), *I Wouldn't Thank You for a Valentine* (Viking, 1992), *The New Republic* (USA), *The New Welsh Review, New Women Poets* (Bloodaxe Books, 1990), *The Paris Review* (USA), *Parnassus* (USA), *Planet, Poetry London Newsletter, Poetry Review, Poetry Wales* and *Verse*.

'Looking for the Celts' was among the finalists of the 1987 *TLS/* Cheltenham Poetry Competition. 'Pentecost' was written as part of the Poetry Squantum at the 1992 Hay-on-Wye Festival of Literature.

Contents

Pentecost

The Lord wants me to go to Florida.
I shall cross the border with the mercury thieves,
as foretold in the faxes and prophecies,
and the checkpoint angel of Estonia
will have alerted the uniformed birds
to act unnatural and distract the guards

so I pass unhindered. My glossolalia
shall be my passport – I shall taste the tang
of travel on the atlas of my tongue –
salt Poland, sour Denmark and sweet Vienna,
and all men in the Spirit shall understand
that, in His wisdom, the Lord has sent

a slip of a girl to save great Florida.
I'll tear through Europe like a standing flame,
not pausing for long, except to rename
the occasional city; in Sofia
thousands converted and hundreds slain
in the Holy Spirit along the Seine.

My life is your chronicle; O Florida
revived, look forward to your past
and prepare your perpetual Pentecost
of golf course and freeway, shopping mall and car
so the fires that are burning in the orange groves
turn light into sweetness and the huddled graves

are hives of the future – an America
spelt plainly, translated in the Everglades
where palm fruit hang like hand grenades
ready to rip whole treatises of air.
Then the S in the tail of the crocodile
will make perfect sense to the bibliophile

who will study this land, his second Torah.
All this was revealed. Now I wait for the Lord
to move heaven and earth to send me abroad
and fulfil His bold promise to Florida.
As I stay put, He shifts His continent:
Atlantic closes, the sheet of time is rent.

The Hedge

With hindsight, of course, I can see that the hedge
was never my cleverest idea
and that bottles of vodka are better not wedged

like fruit in its branches, to counter the fears
and the shakes in the morning on the way to work.
Looking back, I can see how I pushed it too far

when I'd stop in the lay-by for a little lurk
before plunging my torso in, shoulder high
to the hedgerow's merciful root-and-branch murk

till I'd felt out my flattie and could drink in the dry
and regain my composure with the cuckoo-spit.
Then, with growing wonder, I'd watch the fungi,

lovely as coral in the aqueous light.
Lovely, that is, till that terrible day
when the hedge was empty. Weakened by fright

I leant in much deeper to feel out which way
the bottle had rolled and, cursing my luck
(hearing already what my bosses would say

about my being caught in this rural ruck),
I started to panic, so I tussled and heaved
and tried to stand upright, but found I was stuck.

I struggled still harder, but you'd scarcely believe
the strength in a hedge that has set its mind
on holding a person in its vice of leaves

and this one was proving a real bind.
With a massive effort, I took the full strain
and tore up the hedgerow, which I flicked up behind

me, heavy and formal as a wedding train.
I turned and saw, to my embarrassment,
that I'd pulled up a county with my new-found mane,

which was still round my shoulders, with its tell-tale scent
of loam and detritus, while trunk roads and streams
hung off me like ribbons. It felt magnificent:

minerals hidden in unworked seams
shone like slub silver in my churned-up trail.
I had brooches of newly built housing schemes

and sequins of coruscating shale;
power-lines crackled as they changed their course
and woodsmoke covered my face like a veil.

Only then did I feel the first pangs of remorse.
Still, nobody'd noticed so, quickly, I knelt,
took hold of the landscape, folded and forced

it up to a chignon which I tied with my belt.
It stayed there, precarious. The occasional spray
of blackthorn worked loose, but I quickly rebuilt

the ropy construction and tucked it away.
Since then I've become quite hard to approach:
I chew mints to cover the smell of decay

which is with me always. Food tastes of beech
and I find that I have to concentrate
on just holding the hairstyle since it's started to itch

and the people inside it are restless of late.
Still, my tresses have won me a kind of renown
for flair and I find my hair titillates

certain men who want me to take it down
in front of them, slowly. But with deepening dread
I'm watching my old self being overgrown

while scruples rustle like quadrupeds,
stoat-eyed, sharp-toothed in my tangled roots
(it's so hard to be human with a hedge on your head!).

Watch me. Any day I'll be bearing fruit,
sweet hips that glint like pinpricks of blood
and my dry-land drowning will look quite cute

to those who've never fallen foul of wood.
But on bad days now I see nothing but hedge,
my world crazed by the branches of should,

for I've lost all centre, have become an edge
and though I wear my pearls like dew
I feel that I've paid for my sacrilege

as I wish for my autumn with its broader view.
But for now I submit. With me it will die,
this narrowness, this slowly closing eye.

The Voledom of Skomer

For thirty years a suburban naturalist
has studied the life of the SKOMER VOLE
as a pattern of *rodent parochial.*
His colleagues consider him a purist,
look down on his subject as insular,
but he's entranced by the phenomena of local
and all things SKOMER are his exotica.

He's made a fetish of specificity:
the Ramsey field vole's all very well
and yes, he quite likes the pipistrelle,
but the SKOMER VOLE? – Passionate loyalty
and an endless interest in the ins and outs
of a vole that is wholly residual,
one that missed, as it were, the mainland boat

and, surrounded by water, took a snack and just stayed.
In secret he cherishes a mythic version:
the Ur-Vole, a Moses, leads an excursion
across the causeway on a vole crusade
down the slopes of the slippery Continental Shelf
to Skomer and visionary seclusion,
to the safety of his supernatural self.

In the field he's a hawk-eyed devotee,
finding births, deaths and couplings a revelation,
for one man's life spans many generations
of SKOMER VOLE nations and dynasties.
He stoops like a question while, above him, the sky
tries in vain to touch his imagination;
clouds on their columns of rain pass him by,

for he's not drawn to the world by grandeur
but by hours of waiting for the flash of a tail,
for that blur in the dune grass that might be a male.
No, he's wooed through his voleish sense of wonder,
tied by attention to a piece of land
that he feels, one evening, might just set sail
for its observant and most loving husband.

Illinois Idylls

*No idyll's reached
without the gravest
difficulty.*

1

The Boeing dreams its boarding passengers
which are poured, like poison, through its weeping ear.

Jet mushrooms spore their speed in troposphere,
staining the skies above the glacier

where evening's amber and the sea wind blurs
the iceberg galaxies. A drinker stirs

her cocktail and gulps down her time.
Nothing she sees around her can redeem

the tawdry earrings of her whiskey tears,
for she is addicted to the 'over there',

flies blind through high cathedrals
while, below, a city's bar chart reappears:

a human experiment in scrapers' stairs,
temples, ziggurats. Results Not Known.

She has drunk the compass, but its north swings home
and the bride in her veil of Ativan

grows lovelier as the ground draws near
for she is contracted to vertiginous air,

that is, till the runway's shattered shear
shall make her walk out the shining shards of here.

2 *The Correctional Centre*

sets out to make our refractions straight.
Its corridors of bevelled glass
take, like water, the inmates' weight,
for each of us lives by a different gravity.

The building ripples. Liquid hexagons
lap and unloop along pallid walls.
Legs bend mid-muscle. The Centre's halls
are submerged in institutional remorse.

We wade through wisdom. Herons take flight
when we startle them with the boiler room light
and its mangrove sweetness. This new element
is love's surprising geometry

for we are reformed of our rectitude
(of that tree at A-2, that bird at B-3)
and are fully committed to curvature
so that when, at last, we're let out of here

we'll see the world buckle and the highway's rod
ruck to infinity, for buoyancy
has made pliant my spirit. And when I observe
the cats' eyes' blessings, I speed up and then... SWERVE!

*For love gives
us life in a
different
element...*

3

This summer we got our own turning lane,
which makes coming to visit from Rural Route Six
a good deal less dangerous.
Change gear as you enter. Take in the cool
and golden shimmer of the driveway's trees,
avoiding land turtles, startling the quail.

Outside it's like an aquarium.
We sleep by kind currents of leafy light
while humming birds suckle on all that's sweet
and sapsuckers tap on our window panes,
waking us subtly from dry-land dreams.
No idyll is real without jealousy.

We dive down to breakfast. What others breathe
is to us unfamiliar. All that we need
is time and each other, for we conjugate
our love into children, and their children in turn
call us to danger in the shattering sun
outside, where it takes all our strength not to drown.

...so let us
live out odes
to simplicity.

4 *Homecoming*

Two rivers deepening into one;
less said, more meant; a field of corn
adjusting to harvest; a battle won

by yielding; days emptied to their brim;
an autumn; a wedding; a logarithm;
self-evidence earned, a coming home

to something brand new but always known;
not doing, but being – a single noun;
now in infinity; a fortune found

in all that's disposable; not out there, but in,
the ceremonials of light in the rain;
the power of being nothing, but sane.

Even the wood
pile is whole,
with its
hidden snake.

5

God damn it, it's gone and done it again
and I didn't see it! I was up with the dawn,
hoping to catch the house and the farm

reforming themselves to integrity.
But nothing. Even the shagbark hickory
was back to where it was yesterday

though I saw it melting and being undone
last evening, exploding into the dark and random
disintegration of all daylight's forms

till it lost all its treeness in a whirling roar
that surrounded the kitchen. I don't know how we dare
presume our pathways will always be there

or how we imagine that from day to day
we'll recognise husbands or the Milky Way,
as they're ruined and righted for our ignorant gaze,

pushed through time's twisters and night's tornadoes,
each atom returning to a shape it once knew
and the morning's still rising – at least, for now!

The katydids
still calling
have failed to
find a mate.

6

Once I went after the whip-poor-will.
I was tired of hearing such a haunting call
without knowing the caller. So, armed with a torch
I left all the others on the netted porch
and set out in the crackling electric night.

I paused in a clearing. Around me arose
six callers, six fountains, six triangles of song
so lost and alluring they made me long
for myself and for a glimpse of the source
of such ravishing radar, seen face to face.

But whip-poor-wills are ventriloquists
of distance and difficult to place
in the dark and deciduous paradise
of night, calls falling around me like leaves,
the cicada my beacon, soft moths my eyes.

For each time a bird would call out its name
(as if it knew itself) I'd stumble and slide
towards it, hoping to use the beam
of my torch to locate it and pin it there,
beak open, eye glinting, blind but aware

that it had been seen and was fully known.
But it never happened. I stood alone
and the tracer atoms of the fireflies
prickled my skin as I took my fill
of the absent, still-calling whip-poor-will.

*All men should
listen for
the wind beneath
the water.*

7

This pond is full to the brim of itself,
with bullfrogs roaring their geiger applause
for nothing much happening; green darner patrols
with their dry-paper whirring; fish in the trees
and the water rippling its repeated breeze
of reflection weather.

From the bank we watch the pond like a prayer
transforming itself: how molecules of air
are forced through the fringes as the water fights
its own plenty with hunger in the calamus
and everything changes to stay the same.
The dogs hush up and watch the dusk with us.

The currents are coloured scarves round our legs –
forget about air, about human words
for, seen through the surface, the trees iridesce.
Swim in communion as the bats swoop down,
as the woods grow closer, brilliant with gloom
to show us, returning, our best way home.

8

This morning I saw two dinosaurs
locked in combat, their silhouette
heraldic as they held their claws
rampant, two cardinals at war
over their seed, their histories.

Dragons are everywhere. They feed
on cicada fountains, suck dry the roots
and etymologies of trees
to a wordless electricity
turned up by heat to the tautest degree.

We live in ignorance: a child
digs in the dirt for mammoth bones
his father has planted while, over the hill
time turns reptilian and the aeons roll
as the turtle bites down and kisses its kill.

*O give us the
strength for the
long journey from
'she' to 'I'.*

9 *Aunt and Uncle*

You two are the good place
where the others come
to celebrate company on the lawn
with illegal fireworks.
Lightning marbles the suburban sky;
Champaign Urbana is far away
and forgotten as the friends sit down
on rugs and deckchairs and dogs run round
sniffing each other.
The show begins and we applaud
the yellow hornets and coloured pearls
that, any moment, might bring the cops –
colours that make the boys' shadows leap
as far as the driveway;
you watching the light,
me watching you,
so happy the chigres forgot to bite
and mosquitoes were silent
as the spirit pushed
all forms of noxiousness
away for a moment;
nearby in the corn
as the moon grew great
and the night like day
a radio sang to itself and the 'coons,
blasting out Big Band
to the Milky Way.

We are spheres
that are forced
to live in a
line.

10 *Hike to the Vine*

First, we all defied gravity
by scaling a toppled hickory
from roots to branches: dogs barked like birds
and we laughed like leaves at the clarity
of the fallen angles and the rotting tree.

Then we crossed the creek and took on space,
crashed through patches of sassafras,
for men, unlike water, take the longest route
to reason, so we ditched all things straight
and sidled our way though the leaf-crazed light

to the vine, where we were ambushed by time.
The boys climbed up and hung like fruit
and swung, each in turn, like a pendulum
over us adults, weighed down by shadow
and the knowledge that moving clocks run slow.

*Two-thirds water
calls to three-
quarters sea.*

11

Webbed feet run in the family,
skin holds to its tribal memory
of waves and peace in a rising sea.

As babies we float and fall asleep;
where others find water thin and grope
for safety, we trust the deep

and know how to find the water's grain.
Where others flounder, we recline
and find instinctively the line

of least resistance through the river's steel.
We slip inside the current's wheels,
emerge in robes of trailing pearls

till we dive to silence. God of buoyancy,
give us more breath so that we may be
athletes in Your sufficiency.

*For truly this
moment is a world
without end.*

12

These snapshot idylls shall outlast their weather:
the cousins like gases, rearranged on the lawn,
inert and reacting, are rhymes to each other
and reason. See the lilac moon,

it's a dress for their mother, should she put it on
and live out the moment of a luna moth
whose sails shall unfurl in the gale-force sun
that will break them. We are words in the mouth

of daylight, are undone by the dark.
But ride on the present and cousins shall live
in plenitude to the camera's click
which gives its quick blessings to all we receive.

A Golf-Course Resurrection

Mid morning, above the main road's roar
the fairway's splendid – eighteen holes
high on a mountain, which should be all slope,
too steep for a stretch of evenness or poise.
By logic this layout shouldn't work at all
but all the best places are untenable
and the greens are kind as mercy, the course
an airy, open paradox.

The golfers move like penitents,
shouldering bags and counting strokes
towards the justices of handicap and par.
The wind, as sharp as blessing, brings its own tears.
Just out of sight is the mess below:
deconsecrated chapels, the gutted phurnacite,
tips reshaped by crustacean JCBs,
tracts of black bracken that spent the night on fire.

There is a light of last things here.
These men have been translated from the grime
of working the furnace with its sulphur and fire
into primary colours and leisurewear.

They talk of angles, swings and spins.
Their eyes sprout crows' feet as they squint to see
parabolas and arcs, an abstract vision, difficult to learn,
harder to master, but the chosen ones
know what it is to play without the ball
when – white on white – against the Beacons' snow
the point goes missing, yet they carry on
with a sharper focus on their toughest hole,
steer clear of the bunkers, of their own despair,
sinking impossible shots with the softest of putts
still accurate, scoring an albatross
as around them the lark and the kestrel ride
on extravagant fountains of visible air.

Looking for the Celts

The Duchess of Mecklenburg straightens her back,
surveys her fellow enthusiasts,
all digging in soft Salzkammergut rain.
She swaps her mattock for a favourite pick,
glances up at the Hallstatt peak
then, rested, tackles the grave again.

He's close. She can smell him. With trembling hands,
she sorts bone splinters and pottery shards,
sets them aside with the Celtic coins.
She drops to her knees, forgetting her crew,
scrambles, then gives a triumphant cry
as she touches his chest, his barbarian loins.

The *Duchess of Mecklenburg* was one of those
responsible for excavating the Celtic salt mines
in Hallstatt, Austria, at the turn of the century.

A Soviet Waiter

(for Viveka)

I am a Soviet waiter
with buttocks hard and tight.
I lord it over the populace
from my dictatorial height.

My mercy's a measure of vodka
served with a swish of the hand.
When foreigners get stroppy
I pretend I don't understand.

I'm supremely indifferent to smiling,
I'm scarcity's entrepreneur.
You're demand, I'm supply – so remember
normality's saboteur.

Convenience is my currency,
discomfort my stock-in-trade.
When grown men start to beg for food
I know I've got it made.

The odd benign dictator
slips through our swinging doors,
but it's never long till we move him along
and he's polishing corridor floors.

Forget your ideals of service,
I'm hunger and hope's new tsar.
I may not vote in elections
but I carry the samovar.

I feed on the diners' waiting,
grow fat on their silent rage.
Bugger the boys in the Kremlin,
this is the waiter's age.

[Tallinn, 1989]

28

Six Poems on Nothing

I *Midwinter Marriage*

After autumn's fever and its vivid trees,
infected with colour as the light died back,
we've settled to greyness: fields behind gauze,

hedges feint in tracing-paper mists,
the sun diminished to a midday moon
and daylight degraded to the monochrome

of puritan weather. This healing cold
holds us to pared-down simplicities.
Now is the worst-case solstice time,

acutest angle of the shortest day,
a time to condemn the frippery of leaves
and know that trees stand deltas to the sky

producing nothing. A time to take your ease
in not knowing, in blankness, in vacuity.
This is the season that has married me.

II *Annunciation*

When first he painted the Virgin the friar filled
the space around her with angels' wings,
scalloped and plated, with skies of gold,

heavy with matter. He thought that he knew
that heaven was everywhere. He grew
older, wiser and found that he drew

more homely rooms with pots and beds,
but lavished his art on soft furnishings
and the turn of the waiting angel's wings

(still gorgeous with colour and precious dust).
Much later, he sensed that his God had withdrawn,
was spacious. On smaller frescoes he painted less,

let wall be wall, but drew in each lawn
the finer detail of sorrel and weed.
Still later, he found his devotion drawn

to nothing – shadows hinted at hidden rooms,
at improbable arches, while the angel's news
shattered the Virgin, who became a view

as open as virtue, her collapsing planes
easy and vacant as the evening breeze
that had brought a plain angel to his grateful knees.

III

I've made friends with nothing and have found
it is a husband. See these wedding rings?
Two eyes through which I see everything

but not as I used to. Importance leaves me cold,
as does all information that is classed as 'news'.
I like those events that the centre ignores:

small branches falling, the slow decay
of wood into humus, how a puddle's eye
silts up slowly, till, eventually,

the birds can't bathe there. I admire the edge;
the sides of roads where the ragwort blooms
low but exotic in the traffic fumes;

the scruffy ponies in a scrubland field
like bits of a jigsaw you can't complete;
the colour of rubbish in a stagnant leat.

These are rarest enjoyments, for connoisseurs
of blankness, an acquired taste,
once recognised, impossible to shake,

this thirst for the lovely commonplace.
It's offered me freedom, so I choose to stay.
And I thought my heart had been given away.

IV

He started to transform himself in sixty-three,
though few of us knew it at the very start
or suspected his goal was transparency.

We only noticed that he'd disappear
from time to time off the factory floor.
We covered, but his absences grew longer

till, for all our lying, he was finally caught
by the foreman in the locker room,
tied up in a clear chrysalis of thought.

Nothing would shift him, so he got the sack,
but took it quite calmly. When I walked him home
he explained that there was no turning back

from his self-translation. The scales of a butterfly
aren't coloured at all, but are shingles of white
which simply accept the prismatics of light

in spectacular patterns. That humility
was what he was after. I met him often
and watched his skin's translucency

deepen with practice, so that his derm
and epidermis were transmogrified.
He was able to earn some cash on the side

as a medical specimen while muscles and veins
were still visible and then even more
for the major organs as he became pure

through his praying (this after his wife
had sued him for lack of comfort and joy
in their marriage) but by then his life

was simply reflective. I could only discern
his shape in the sunshine, so purged was he
of his heaviness and opacity.

He knew he was nothing. Through him I saw
colours shades deeper than ever before
and detail: the ratchets on a snail's rough tongue,

the way light bruises, how people fall
to weakness through beauty and when we came
to him for vision, he accepted us all,

made us more real, gave us ourselves
redeemed in the justice of his paraphrase,
the vivid compassion of his body's gaze.

V *'A Calm'*

Nothing is happening everywhere,
if only we knew it. Take these clouds,
our most expensive purchase to date,

five million for a fleet becalmed
off the coast of nowhere. I like the restraint
that chose this lack of action in paint,

this moment of poise between travel and rain –
cumulonimbus in a threatening sky,
horizon, cumulonimbus again

as water gives the air its rhyme
and the pressure keeps dropping. An oily tide
buoys up a barrel by the coaster's side,

emptied, no doubt, by the sailors on board
waiting, tipsy, for their lives to begin
again with the weather. The clouds close in

but this boredom's far richer than anything
that can happen inside it – than the wind, than a port,
or the storm that will wipe out this moment of nought.

'A Calm': a painting by Jan van de Capelle,
newly acquired by the National Museum of Wales.

VI

The monk says nothing, finger to his lips
and day begins inside his silences.
First dawn then birdsong fill the gaps

his love has left them. He's withdrawn
to let things happen. His humility
has allowed two kinds of ordinary –

sparrows and starlings – to fight it out
over the fruit of a backyard tree
and against the blackbirds. His nonentity

is a fertile garden, fed from the well
of a perfect cipher, and the water's cool,
most nourishing. He drinks his fill

and cities happen in his fissured mind,
motorways, roadblocks. He is host
to ecosystems that sustain us all,

for our lives depend on his emptiness.
His attention flickers. He turns away
to something and destroys our day.

Squaring the Circle

Mary of Burgundy (1457-1482)

Philip the Handsome (1478-1505) = *Joanna the Mad* (1479-1555)

Here is the body
of Mary of Burgundy
with a box containing the heart
of her son,
Philip the Handsome.
Was it wise
to become
so centralised?

In a convent in Spain
Joanna the Mad,
enflamed by all
the women he had,
keeps guard at his body
inflamed by the heat
of the gothic fever
that's to be her fate –
her Castilian hate.
For who's to say
where his real heart lay?

And in the Salle des Mariages
the members of Mary's entourage
have been hung like portraits,
so they never think
of rearranging this odd ménage
of three dominions
all out of synch.

For these
are not bodies
but polities
and the truth is
that having Philip back
has given his mother
a heart attack.

The Soul Mine

The guidebook directed us to a nunnery
where no one spoke English.
Nearby, a quarry
was blasting for granite,
working to free
buildings and walls from the rockery
of rubble. In a dark chapel
a nun, almost silent, mined the air
making a statue of breathing and prayer.

Heroic sisters! They are the quarry
of a spirit that hunts them.
Love is predatory,
best met with stillness
and passivity.
The smashed heart is its own safety.
Water flows, soft, from the rock.
Minds and minerals submit to their loads:
cold stones that women kiss explode.

A Fanciful Marriage

So it came that Too Little married Too Much
and all pronounced it an ideal match,
as tending towards the golden mean:

a chance for Too Much to be somewhat less,
for Too Little to wax into something more.
The priest and the guests felt sure it was blessed.

'O cup to my water, be my weather vane!'
'Rain to my drought, you are hurricane!'
They looked lovely in matching metonymies.

But they left out one guest – the Literal –
who sneaked, unseen, into the hall
to utter her matter-of-fact revenge:

'See things as they are, for only a fool
can pretend a cracked cup can ever be full
or that mankind can catch it when brightness falls.'

For a while they were fine. Too Little grew fat
and, filling out to his marriage vows,
abandoned his famine in favour of feast.

But his viscera got him. No conjugal bliss
could stop him from turning away in disgust.
Soon he had slid into someone less,

past least, until he was merely some,
an honest-to-goodness matchstick man –
he'd tried to be golden, but had ended up mean.

Too Much grew rampant at his mutiny
and ditched her honeymoon regime
to rail against the insults of time.

Dressed in gowns of bitter glory,
she flung floods at her husband's thing of stone,
wove storms of illusion, but woke alone

to worry the winds to their proper paths,
and hold up huge cities by force of will,
keeping coal to its seams beneath the hills.

But all was not lost for, during a lull,
he lifted his siege, she breached his wall
and they had a bit of the actual.

Surprise! A daughter! and on her face
the seven letters of 'Homo Dei'
spelt promise, reliance and simple grace

(if only they'd seen it). So, day by day,
their hopes grew high on her infant health,
bridge of their bloods, their commonwealth,

the map that would chart their antipodes!
The Literal sighed and the child fell asleep
between her parents' parentheses.

She grew and they redrew their battle lines
to criss-cross their daughter, who lived in fear
that she'd always fall short of their metaphors.

A blank, she became the board for their games:
The words on her face were never the same
as they played hard scrabble with desperate hands...

compliance, no, defiance. These shifting sands
blunted her features, dulled her hair
as she mimicked cold triumph or old despair,

sure that her mirror could save their souls.
Till her own went missing. Then, how she ran,
chasing its radiant flickering

down alleys of phantasmagoria
that ravish travellers from what they are,
dim waters that make the near far

and all holding impossible, where the past
takes hostages to make itself last.
Still her satellite danced ahead,

glinting through chasms, past chimeras
that flayed her of feeling and left her for dead.
Her parents grew anxious and, quiet with dread,

went looking for her, hand in hand.
Together they tried to understand
how their marriage had slid so wide of the mark.

Too Little wept and Too Much let him be....
They finally found her where a troupe of tropes
had turned her to pure geometry.

High in electric air she hung
too like a triangle to hear
how they wanted her down from the sizzling wire;

and around the echoing chamber
resplendent reflections glided and glanced
away from the empty darkness of her.

They stood transfixed, their faces two noughts.
'Come down!' called Too Little, but his daughter's pain
wound her up tighter and started a spin.

But somehow she'd glimpsed their frightened eyes,
a spirit level to her tilting skies.
She stirred but, held back by stunning bolts,

described another sickening arc
for she had remembered and brittle tears
fell in a brilliant shower of sparks.

'Help her', they prayed to the Literal,
'save her from this human fall,
for we can do nothing for her as we are.'

At that the uninvited guest
stepped from the shadows and gently unbound
the girl from her cradle and bore her down

softly and, as the floor drew near,
she whispered: 'There's nothing further to fear
for I am your gravity and your grace,

the only contentment you'll ever know.
So remember this twisted parable of you.
Our lives begin as you touch the ground.'

And she set her down and, patient and mild,
showed them each other, then took them home –
a father, a mother, and a shaking child.

FROM **Welsh Espionage**

V

Welsh was the mother tongue, English was his.
He taught her the body by fetishist quiz,
father and daughter on the bottom stair:
'Dy benelin yw *elbow*, dy wallt di yw *hair*,

chin yw dy ên di, *head* yw dy ben.'
She promptly forgot, made him do it again.
Then he folded her *dwrn* and, calling it fist,
held it to show her knuckles and wrist.

'Let's keep it from Mam, as a special surprise.
Lips are *gwefusau*, *llygaid* are eyes.'
Each part he touched in their secret game
thrilled as she whispered its English name.

The mother was livid when she was told.
'We agreed, no English till four years old!'
She listened upstairs, her head in a whirl.
Was it such a bad thing to be Daddy's girl?

VII *The Spy Comes Home*

Leave, if you like, but those you've left won't wait
to bear you witness once you've broken free.
Now pay the price for coming home too late.

Warmth I expected, or a loving hate,
the deserter resented for his liberty.
Leave, if you like, but those you've left won't wait.

Peer through the window at the leaded grate,
tap on the pane with the rain-soaked tree.
Now pay the price of coming home too late.

Steal away and time will confiscate
the place you hoarded in your memory.
Leave, if you like, but those you've left won't wait.

Who's to redeem the jaded reprobate,
if not the incurious in the family?
Now pay the price of coming home too late.

A row of graves by the chapel gate,
mouths as cold as their charity.
Leave, if you like, but those you've left won't wait.
Now pay the price of coming home too late.

IX *Advice on Adultery*

The first rule is to pacify the wives
if you're presented as the golden hope
at the office party. You're pure of heart,
but know the value of your youthful looks.
Someone comments on your lovely back.
Talk to the women, and avoid the men.

In work they treat you like one of the men
and soon you're bored with the talk of the wives
who confide in you about this husband's back,
or that husband's ulcer. They sincerely hope
you'll never have children...it ruins your looks.
And did you know David has a dicky heart?

You go to parties with a beating heart,
start an affair with one of the men.
The fact you've been taking more care of your looks
doesn't escape the observant wives
who stare at you sourly. Cross your fingers and hope
that no one's been talking behind your back.

A trip to the Ladies. On your way back
one of them stops you for a heart to heart.
She hesitates, then expresses the hope
that you won't take offence, but men will be men,
and a young girl like you, with such striking looks....
She's heard nasty rumours from some of the wives.

She knows you're innocent, but the wives,
well, jump to conclusions from the way it looks....
In a rage you resolve she won't get him back,
despite the pressure from the other wives.
They don't understand... you'll stick with the men,
only they are *au fait* with affairs of the heart.

You put it to him that you're living in hope.
He grants that you're beautiful, but looks
aren't everything. He's told the men,
who smirk and wink. So now you're back
to square one, but with a broken heart.
You make your peace with the patient wives.

Don't give up hope at the knowing looks.
Get your own back, have a change of heart:
Ignore the men, start sleeping with the wives.

XI

So this is the man you dreamt I had betrayed.
I couldn't have saved him if I'd stayed.

He's old as his language. On his bony knees
his hands are buckled like wind-blown trees

that were straight in his youth. His eyes are dim,
brimming with water. If you talk to him

he'll mention people whom you never knew,
all in their graves. He hasn't a clue

who you are, or what it is you want
on your duty visits to Talybont.

This is how languages die – the tongue
forgetting what it knew by heart, the young

not understanding what, by rights, they should.
And vital intelligence is gone for good.

The Bad Shepherd

Cornelius Varro knows his husbandry
and he maintains a flourishing estate:
'My mutes stand guard at the entrance gate.
Vowels I lodge with my hired men,
half-vowels sit by the cattle pen.
Of course, I let the spirants work the field,
as they're teaching the clover how to yield
to consonantal chimings from the church.'
But I'm uncouth and keep lip service back.

For I'm the one who herds his fields of wheat,
speaks softly till the stalks are white,
the ripe ears heavy. Then I sow my spite
and laugh to see how the rows stampede,
as I spread sedition with the highland wind
till they're wrecked and broken. Then he sends men round
and I watch in silence as they slowly reap
his yearly tribute from my grudging ground.

Going Primitive

Who can resist a didgeridoo
in the middle of Queen St – not one, but three
from the Northern Territory,
each one more deeply, eucalyptically rude?

For the builders have lost the passers-by
who are drawn like water to the swirl and squelch,
the monstrous plumbing of his breath,
sucked in and further, and then atomised,

breathed out in stiff shirts and office skirts
but feeling looser....
A wasp photographer
hassles the man for something sweet

and the women, who sweat at his embouchure,
grow broad as rivers to his narrow lips,
dirty as deltas, with silting hips
and alluvial bosoms. The men, unsure,

cower behind their totem wives,
puny and trouty; now chimpanzees
swing through the scaffolding with ease
and screech with the newly arrived macaws;

cranes buck and bow and the wooden thrum
makes men recall a biography
of sludge and savannah, how it was when the sky
arched its blue back and started to come.

The Reference Library

(to open the sixth-form library at Ysgol Gyfun Rhydfelen)

Elsewhere a leather-bound volume holds the sum
of what a distant century knew
about cosmology and Christendom,
of how to cook with feverfew,

how to make silk, how Latin spread
like roads across a kingdom which then fell
to rhetoric and laws and lead
but let prophetic fishes tell

their older stories, ones of mortal sin,
when men of rock were spawned from tors
with tongues of granite, breathing whin
which stopped the logical conquerors.

How comprehensive! Look around you now:
concordances are a thumbnail wide,
a wafer-thin thesaurus shows you how
new languages are regicides;

there are directories of heads of state,
files of disease with their listed cures,
transport technologies to contemplate,
anatomies of the urban poor....

But compared to you, an encyclopaedia
is thin provision. Throw the big tomes out,
and the almanacs with their logorrhoea.
Read first the lexicons of your own doubt,

for in your spines and not in those of books
lies the way to live well, the best library;
for the erudition of your open looks
shall make old words forge new theologies.

Parables and Faxes

The hum was there from before the start:
my mother, a baby, on her sister's lap
and the hive behind them, its whitewashed slats
squat as a stanza. I can feel its heat

and the sepia blur of a landing bee
dancing the scents of a stamen he came
to offer in steps to the greedy comb
and trade in the world for geometry.

We are all transformers: we change what we see
into sap and succour; the hive's a machine
that hoards up the substance for its working soul,
a Madonna of amber and electricity.

And now in my dreams the neutrinos sing
from a hive in the corner and the atom's halls
are held up by talking, by great upheavals
and voices so truthful that snatches heard fling

all sense into terror, the square room round,
the set world bucking. What is this grace
which keeps knowing so near us, but the lid in place,
that insists on the gift of a throbbing ground?

After a winter out in the cold
the tramp was honking.

They broke open the seals with trembling hands.

In death he looked almost beautiful
but was foul when he woke for his photograph
at the start of his treatment.

They were scared by the glint of guardian eyes
till they knew them for statues.

So bad was the smell that they cut off his clothes
and burned them, ceremoniously.

From that moment they knew this prince was great...

Fungus grew out of the doctors' mouths
and the nurses breathed flowers...

...for his flesh was tectonic plates of gold
and under that honey, black with the burn
of all those millennia...

...Heminevrin and Temazepam....

...the omnipotent tibia shattered by air,
his fingers sticking to the scarab rings,
his pelvis plundered....

Much later, they danced in their dressing-gowns
under the moon of the white clock's face
and the horns of Isis, no cords and no belts,
profile Pharaonic, with a Nubian grace,
pouring libations from dementia's wine.
The resurrected, they have swallowed time.

We lived off the Street of Incendiaries
the winter the city finally fell
and yielded to the infidel.

Our Lord, the Elephant of God,
was captured and tortured by slow degrees
as the city lost its integrity.

The arrows of the mercenaries
rained on us like germs, till the crumbling walls
succumbed at last to the siege's disease.

But I remember our immunity:
the starlings' static in sighing trees,
the flames of caged canaries,

green courtyards, bromeliads licking the light
from under the tamarinds; and Mary's crown
like snakes, her wrath our fortune,

and the cool burn of her composure
the dark centre of our best desires,
our safety lodged in her danger.

Forgive us. Now, on St Lucy's Day,
we offer the ruined city in praise
back to the sun, and the strengthening sky

so the broken begin to prophesy
through solstice and slaughter to a citadel
that none but the routed shall ever occupy.

It's impossible, but it's happening:

Your face, a river, runs from yesterday;
your words, a fountain, fall back into sleep

to rise and break out in deliberate rain.
You are poise and pivot and swing the moon

on its cantilever till the known skies tilt
into reflection. You are blindness felt,

the gravity pull of absent light,
the seed inside the sacrament.

You're all that's easy, all that flies in the face
of the will that prefers its flowers forced

while I...I am unravelling twine
whose brokenness is laid in time

to give purchase to crystals till my spacious halls
can house you and the raven's call,

so still in the grove you could drink your fill
of blackness from its brimming well.

Saxons are vertical,
circles we,
hence the mutual hostility.
They climb, we spiral;
who shall be
the better in their eternity?

Curls tend to churls
while ladders rise;
they are legs and we the eyes
that watch the progress of the earls
across the skies
over the clods they patronise.

We are return
but progress they,
roundabout versus motorway.
We borrow but they always own
the deeds of day,
certificates for right of way.

A thane is bright,
no plodder he,
an apex of geometry
that draws the Angles to their heights;
though fantasy
must know the fear of gravity.

The humble are fly
and know the crown
for an O in which a man can drown
or drink his death – such irony
is for the prone
who must praise the good they'll never own.

She wants to be transported all the time
but has fallen further than the theatre floor,
the girl whose pain moves like a *pas-de-deux*,
the sordid partnering the sublime.

The world falls upwards – beat it down
with booze and *bourrées*, *entrechats* and speed;
for the perfect *jeté* and the sharp aside
disguise the danger of the looming ground

once you have climbed your staircases of air
and blown your back-ups and you see, below,
how car tops look like plumped-up pillows
and – here it comes – concrete like an easy chair.

So the Lord said: 'Eat this scroll.'
I did and it was sweet and light and warm
and filled my belly. But I didn't speak
for all His urgings. Tolstoy's good
and Kafka nourishing. I lick

the fat from all the books I can
in the shops at lunchtime – Ovid, Byron, Keats....
The assistants know me, but they let me feast
on spaghetti sentences if I don't break the spines
of paperbacks and replace them fast

so buyers never know their books
are licked of God. I am voracious
for the Word – a lexicon is wine
to me and wafer, so that home, at night,
I ruminate on all that's mine

inside these messages. I am the fruit
of God's expressiveness to man.
I grow on libraries, suck the grapes
of Os and uncials and still –
no prophecies. When I am ripe

I shall know and *then* you'll see the caravans,
processions, fleets, parades come from my mouth
as I spew up cities, colonies of words
and flocks of sentences with full-stop birds
and then, when I'm empty I shall open wide

and out will come fountains for the chosen few
to bathe in as time falls into brilliant pools,
translucent and ruined. Meantime I shall grow
stony with knowing, and my granite tongue
shall thirst (God's gargoyle!) for these blessings' blows.

Dog Bite Followed by Madness   FAX
(*WESTERN MAIL* HEADLINE, MARCH 1928)

The dog did it and that's definite.
Luther was sound before he was bit
and we still don't believe the magistrate

who found the damned mongrel innocent
of Uncle Luther's mania.
There must have been hydrophobia

(though the records don't show it and the dog was put down).
He was mad when we called the policeman in,
breaking the furniture and raving

with chthonic fury about a Cerberus
who bit him as he tried to pass
through underworld caves to get back to us,

for he was the Rhondda's Persephone.
The dog bite, he howled, would guarantee
his return to inferno, his immortality,

We humoured him and, ranting, he died,
but we always remembered what Luther had said
about havoc and Hades. Now we cross the road

to avoid all guard dogs – a family fear.
For if it wasn't the dog, then it was Luther
and sour-breathed Cerberus is always too near.

King William conquered the British Isles
with griffins and dragons with knots in their tails:
God's order in the borders of time –
centaurs rampant and leopards tame
with the lambs they slaughtered and the crane
kind to the wolf that killed it. Now a wife
opens her arms in a garden, starts a gale
that impregnates the Normans' sails
and brings them in force to Pevensey.
Now the peacock and the harpy cry
out so Saxons die and horses fall
while, in the border, ornament is all
and trees that are rooted in history
hold birds more real than the sights they see
until the wyverns are put to rout
and human bodies blot the border out.

Today set sail like a cruising ship
taking us with it, so we waved goodbye
to the selves that we were yesterday
and left them ashore like a memory
while we launched out on the open sea,
were travelling! The breeze grew stiff
so we grabbed the railings, tasting the surf
as the sky came towards us, the equator noon
a place to pass us, while the tropics of tea
swung over us and straight on by
as time kept sailing and we hung on,
admiring the vistas of being away
while the shadows died down from the flames of day
and we coasted around a long headland of sky
and into night's port while, out in the bay
tomorrow called out like a ringing buoy.

It seemed a simple case of opulence,
when diggers discovered the marble pool
still edged in lapis lazuli and gold
with dolphin mosaics under a portico,
all placed so the swimmer would seem to dive
into the wealth of the valley below.

But mercy's a mystery and takes time to see:
They found another pool outside the gates,
its bottom cluttered with unclaimed lamps
knocked over by lepers as they shuffled, late,
to bathe there in secret, never thinking that now
we see them immersing themselves in pure light.

My God! in the hands of a lunatic
and taken hostage!
One mistake
and he and I could both be dead,
like flies on a windowsill.
He's out of his head

on greed and wanting and he'll do me in
if he's not seen to.
I can never win
this game of blind because I'm the buff.
I supply his demands
but it's never enough

to appease him. He can live for days
on nothing but will
until he's crazed
on making things happen and exchanging fire.
They say I love him
but it's only fear

of life without him, all on my own,
without the excitement
or the charm of a gun
to my head, feeling wanted, part of a 'we',
not perched on a lonely
column of I.

And yet, if I choose, he will fall away,
for a soul is far stronger
than the rampant me
with its threats and its deadlines. Pity his end,
a defeat he will never
understand

while I, undiminished, will carry on,
a nothing, transparent,
not on the run
but moving much faster and able to feel
the speed of travelling
while perfectly still.

Something shifted and the landscape breathed,
killing two thousand – the Angel of the Lord
was with us, bless this deadly Lord

and his fatal Angel who has left, freeze-framed,
these lives in emblem: father holding son,
a mother running. Angel of the Lord,

who stopped the messenger on the dusty road
and spread out his body, a forgotten word
in a dying language. Angel of the Lord,

who undressed the elders as they tried to flee
then took them from their histories,
Angel who teaches that we do not see

but are seen by greatness, held then killed
by the swiftest glance, that those who win
are those who lose the fight with him,

the wrestling Angel, who takes everything,
as is his right: the Angel of the Lord,
wielding the evening breezes as his sword.

This Mahādeva is a great white dog
who sets out with me on a winter walk
in snowy mountains, though he never stays.
He is also the god who suddenly appears
to herd men's souls, a palindrome, a way

of moving, though the world withdraws
from us in mist, as faith draws back from words,
to leave us groping. Hear him pant behind,
circling my path then passing, pulled ahead
by smells that say this is his land

though I keep to the path, as farmers shoot for rain
and other creatures. In the fields around
the melt is making continents of snow
and slopes are shading into mackerel skies
that hide him from me. Now as I go

rain brings down mist and I find that I wear
thousands of diamonds on clothes and hair
and now it's white-out and behind I hear
that Mahādeva the wolf is here,
hungry for wonder, thirsting for fear.

Mahādeva, the 'God who suddenly appears' is a form of
the Hindu god Śiva. A friend's dog is named after him.

Talking of eating, did you see those crows
on the Peñas Grajeras as they gathered at dusk
in their hundreds, till the cliffs were dark

with rifts and gossip? Rook-saturated rock
seethed with a sleekness that shone in the gloom
as if the birds were devouring time

and making the rapid twilight gleam
with calls that drew the moon's wafer near.
This ancient pact is enacted there:

man's failure feeds the ravens' hunger
and they, in time, remind the man
that the filth of his own carrion –

humiliation, lies and pain –
is transformed into manna; then, the watcher, in turn,
sees how the birds of blackness burn

his world to nothing and so he discerns
that shining ruin is his only creed,
and noxious night most necessary bread.

Cliff of Rooks: behind the burial place
of St John of the Cross, Segovia.

She came to me
in a dream of enormous bosoms,
magnificent lallers,
not hers but mine,
that had grown from nothing,
ripened and swelled
till they overflowed my office blouse
and were... a phenomenon.
My colleagues looked on
but no one was rude
about my stupendous amplitude.

Word spread and other workers came
to see for themselves
so I fed them,
telling them all the while
of how it is that all is well
and how endlessly
the miracle welled up in me
of her kindness and generosity.

And then the hall
was filled with my hair
and knowing this
was really her
we swam in the whorls
of her fragrant care

and nobody minded
that no work was done
for Tara held us
in her plenitude,
for her help is warm,
her breath is food!

Tara is a Buddhist deity especially
helpful in overcoming difficulties.

It's seldom we know how lucky we are:
A dragon's head smokes in the darkening air
and talk turns to wonder – how the stars are near,
how life burns the bones of those who are far
in time to embers more fragrant and charred
than the bonfire before us.

                          The dragon roars on,
blotting out sour cherry and lime,
for his sentences blind us – he talks of Beauty
that bound him tight with her terrible calm
and brought him, grotesque, to his gracious knees,
a monster for ever. We feel her take aim
from the shadows and shush as the trees
draw near with our dying days in their arms.

      (1916)

And now I remember the tall hussar
who gave me the halo of telegraph wire
which I wound round my body at the age of six.
Since then my hearing's been strangely acute,
for I watched as the workmen erected a line
of identical crosses all the way down
to the river that kept on discussing itself
out through the village, on to somewhere's sea....
He was huge in his dolman and when he saw

my delight at the splitting and hewing of wood
he called me closer to his brilliant braid;
then the world dipped and I could see the way
that men were cradled in the criss-cross tree,
hammering nonsense, till they left one man
like a Christ on the wire there, hanging alone
but listening to something that no one else heard.
My heart beat in dashes back down on the ground
and I knew that I'd learn how to understand

the metal's despatches. Now, since the war
I've crossed high passes to talk in Morse
to other receivers, leading horses piled high
with the weight of talking, till I found my way
here to the trenches, to the news of troops,
disasters and weather, where now I'm stretched out,
nerves copper and all my circuits aware
they're transmitting a man on a wheel of barbed wire,
nothing but message, still tapping out fire.

For the one
who said yes,
how many
said no?

Of course,
there was
the Sumatran who refused
and then the Nubian,
then the Swede,
who shied away
from bearing the Word,
though the chance
was offered...
a Finn, a Chinese....
Declining politely
they carried on
with the dusting
or with its equivalent
so the question
was left
to an Indian, a Lapp,
petitioned by God
for outrageous assent,
for in sweetest closeness
all being is rent.

But those who said no
for ever knew
they were damned
to the daily
as they'd disallowed
reality's madness,
its astonishment.

So the moment passed
and the fissure closed,
an angel withdrew,
no message sent,
and the lady prepared
her adequate meal –
food of free will –
from which God
a while longer
was absent.

This is the place where the boys get killed –
not underground, where the river flows
in lakes so reflective nobody knows
where dark ends and where new currents begin.
No, this is the danger – where the water flings

itself to the light, so cold it can tear
all breath from a body, as it speaks its words
of strength and revival and opens wide,
looking like reason, persuading the young
whom it drowns in the lies of its treacherous tongue.

And this, too, is love:

The tanker *Cliona* on the Coral Sea,
called in to assist a hospital ship
hit by the Japs and sinking in flames.
The tanker, which carries a cargo of fuel
so flammable hammers are banned on deck,
for fear their sparks might ignite stray gas,
draws near to the liner. Nurses drop down
and patients are winched from the burning hulk
to the *Cliona*, which is carrying death
but Captain O'Hara holds the ship near
to its ultimate danger and the searing heat
blisters their faces – love's garment is pain
and impossible daring. Now the undertow
brings them still closer, the whole crew burns
in anticipation of the moment she blows
but still she doesn't: how long can she last
before physical logic remembers the load?
– each moment's precious, lent from the blast –
before love and its opposite crash and explode?

So the world offers itself in love:
A park on a Sunday with a simple band,
oom–pah–pah under the cherry tree.
What could be more ordinary?

But time divided the music like this:
To open, an easy ball was thrown,
caught with a lunge of the skirt, a laugh,
two children (related) running around
pursued by a dog who can't get enough
of municipal smells from the mellow sound
which starts to repeat – the ball gets thrown,
till, this time, the girl runs round on her own,
followed by dog with a lolloping tongue.

Then the reprise: ball in an arc,
not fumbled now but moving free
from one hand to another, the dog, then three
youngsters (must be one family)
chased by the music; the sun goes in,
world goes flat, dog takes a break,
but the children are back, each one a repeat
with variations and, in their wake,
a blackbird bouncing as crescendo and ball
arch over the moment and let them all through,
toddler chasing the other two,
dog yapping, happy having caught a ball
in the doily shade of the cherry tree
where the baton beat out eternity
for a moment before we went home for our tea.

Not all statues can change allegiances.
These are recusants that have been seized
and brought to this park by the new regime
to be hung by crane for political crimes

and out-of-date gestures. An historical wind
blows iron trousers against communist limbs
from different directions, as men in suits
(there are three Lenins at the entrance gate)

regard naked heroes, all muscle and thrust,
who were happy to bare their collective chests
to lead the people. Now they direct
the starling traffic and orchard troops

into the thick of the afternoon
in which nothing happens, where they gesture alone.
Before they were orators – men were their words
and iron foundries their strongest verbs

though now they avoid each other's eyes
but hear as the workmen take their ease,
smoking behind them, and they're forced to see
a concrete-mixer decide their history.

I saw a vision:
In a place called Pripyat
something exploded
from inside a tomb.
In the next room
someone was washing
as the geigers roared
and despite their scourging
the showers' rods
failed to restore
innocence
to the reactor's core.

The fire spread
and the roof-tops burned
to show where a bride
and her nuclear groom
turned water to wormwood
while men in lead
joined in the dancing,
already dead.

And there, beyond the reactor's walls,
where Judas has hung himself,
Christ explodes
pointing a finger
as the isotopes
massacre children
on the vision's slopes.

And further out
Elijah's birds
feed him with darkness
by the motorway
and men are turned black
by the light of day.

And then, even further,
at the edge of time
Christ is baptised
in a gentle stream
and fish come to nibble,
the stars to see
God become one
with the burning flesh
that falls from men's bones
at the blinding flash
of his slightest appearance,
so the saints come to watch,
their haloes like moons,
burning like sixty thousand moons.

A saint from the east
and a saint from the west
decided to travel so that they met.
The day they appointed the sun was hot
so the saint from the east was burnt on his neck,
the one from the west had a flaming face
when they settled on opposite banks of a stream
for holy conversation.

West was Parable, dazzled by the sun,
crows' feet showing how he used his eyes
to squint and focus, distance and transform
hints from nature into another order
which his imagination could explain.

East was Fax, straight observation,
simple facts lit from afar,
seen in themselves by long attention
and strict devotion to things as they are –
not Parable's similes, but metaphor.

Said Fax to Parable: 'How can you guess
what all you see can begin to mean?'
And Parable back: 'How can *you* bless
the chaotic surface that resists the sign?'

They argued until the sun wheeled round,
throwing two shadow saints on the ground.
Slowly they both began to cool
and language was left on their beards like rime,
their words in scrolls, which dropped from their hands,
as they stood, still struggling to understand
how they could shake off tyrant time
and still the stream laughed past in a line,
praying its way to the lexicon sea,
to nonsense and nonentity.

And then they knew they were bound to fail
and once they knew this they were suddenly full
of a better emptiness, wordless and wide,
which was known and tasted and felt like a flood
of breath in which all sense must lie,

brilliant like bubbles, to be quickly burst.
And they knew this was right by the quenching thirst
which turned them – one with his face to the sun,
the other his neck – and sent them home
to do what they could with provisional praise
and their partial vision, both overcome
by a conversation they'd scarcely begun.